C000044409

Cheshire
and the Gritstone Edge

Compiled by
Neil Coates

Acknowledgements

My thanks to Dave Small, Mike Pole, Bev Ridyard, Geoff Perry and Paul Quare for route checking and even an occasional pertinent comment or observation – and for the odd pint or two along the way.

Text:	Neil Coates
Photography:	Neil Coates
Editorial:	Ark Creative (UK) Ltd
Design:	Ark Creative (UK) Ltd

While every care has been taken to ensure the accuracy of the route directions, the publishers cannot accept responsibility for errors or omissions, or for changes in details given. The countryside is not static: hedges and fences can be removed, field boundaries can alter, footpaths can be rerouted and changes in ownership can result in the closure or diversion of some concessionary paths. Also, paths that are easy and pleasant for walking in fine conditions may become slippery, muddy and difficult in wet weather, while stepping-stones across rivers and streams may become impassable.

If you find an inaccuracy in either the text or maps, please write to Crimson Publishing at the address below.

First published 2003 by Jarrold Publishing. Reprinted 2008

This edition first published in Great Britain 2010 by Crimson Publishing, a division of:

Crimson Business Ltd
Westminster House, Kew Road
Richmond, Surrey, TW9 2ND
www.totalwalking.co.uk

Printed in Singapore. 3/10

Front cover: Roaches Ridge from Wincle Minn
Previous page: Three Shires Head bridge

Contents

Keymap

SCALE 1:416 666 or 1 INCH to about 6½ MILES *1CM to 4.2KM*

0   2   4   6   8   10 KILOMETRES   15

0   2   4   6 MILES 8   10

KEYMAP HEIGHTS SHOWN IN METRES

Introduction

Cheshire

The very name is redolent of rich dairy farming country, dappled with
half-timbered country pubs, quaint black and white villages and herds of
matching Friesian cattle. A land of cheese and butter, salt mines and lazy
rivers; old sandstone churches crowning low hills in a countryside dotted
with sublime country houses amidst vast estates. There is more than a
little truth to the bucolic image of this, one of England's oldest counties
(first recorded in AD980), but there is, too, a great deal more that makes it
ideal walking country. Note that Walks 14 and 18 are in traditional
Cheshire, now ostensibly part of Greater Manchester.

Through the Ages

The Romans recognised that the area we know as Cheshire was a pivotal
location from which they could control much of the north of England
and north Wales. Their city of Deva, a major port and base for their
renowned 20th Legion, is today's Chester.

Those later invaders, the Normans, were equally convinced by the
location and established a County Palatine here, essentially a self-
governing state within England. From here the powerful Marcher Lords
attempted to keep the Welsh under control; many old castle sites dot the
countryside of west Cheshire. In an archaic ceremony, one of the gates
through Chester's City Walls is still locked each night at 21.00 in order to
keep out the troublesome Welsh.

Medieval times saw the development of the salt industry and the rise of
the farming 'agristocracy,' establishing the substantial estates that
characterise much of the county. Many magnificent 'magpie' mansions,
such as Little Moreton Hall and Gawsworth Hall, survive from this time.
These are complemented by huge Georgian and Victorian houses that
often replaced their half-timbered predecessors. The prime example is
the palatial Lyme Hall to the south of Stockport; others include
Capesthorne and Arley.

Nor did the Industrial Revolution pass Cheshire by. The north and east of the county, in particular, were drawn in to the industrialisation that saw the rapid growth of Manchester. The well-established silk industry of Congleton and Macclesfield thrived, while cotton mills gave a new skyline to Bollington and Stockport. Carpets, calico, hats and candlewicks saw virtually every one of Cheshire's Pennine streams worked to the last drop of water. The legacy is a superb array of industrial archaeology, prime among which is the utopian community established at Styal by the visionary industrialist Samuel Greg.

The Cheshire Edges
Many people imagine Cheshire as being a very flat county, an image perhaps confirmed by the views from train windows or motorway-based travel. While there certainly are great tracts of flat land – a prehistoric sea basin scoured and reworked by the great ice sheets 15,000 years ago – it is the sheer variety of Cheshire's countryside that makes the county an ideal one to explore farther on foot.

Budworth Mere

A pronounced ridge of sandstone cuts north – south down the middle of the county. This backbone of Cheshire is riddled with ancient and medieval gems, from the hill forts of Maiden Castle and Eddisbury to the sublime Beeston Castle. In and around Delamere Forest, which cloaks part of the ridge, are the remnants of the great forest of Mara and Mondrum that stretched from Shropshire to the Mersey in early medieval times. The great ramparts of Frodsham and Helsby Hills stand sentinel above the widening estuary of the Mersey as the ridge falters, reappearing intermittently on the Wirral and well into Lancashire.

It is the eastern flank of the county, however, that holds most surprises. This is the final fling of the Pennines and hides as spectacular countryside as can be found anywhere in this famous chain of hills. Fractured ridges of gritstone characterise the area, the gorge-like valleys in between thick with woodland and liberally sprinkled with industrial hamlets and villages that have a character all their own. Windswept grouse moors cloaked with sedges, peat bogs and pools rise to the county's highest point, Shining Tor at 1,834ft (559m). The whole area is criss-crossed by miles of packhorse roads and saltways, the arteries of medieval Cheshire now wonderful routes into this most endearing part of the county, The Gritstone Edge.

Canals

No matter where you are in Cheshire, you won't be far from a canal. The oldest, the Bridgewater, threads across the north. Built in the 1750s to move coal the short distance from mines at Worsley to Manchester, its tentacles soon reached the Mersey at Runcorn and connected to the Grand Trunk Canal (better known as the Trent and Mersey), forerunners of a network that provided an impetus for the industrial and commercial development of England.

The Trent and Mersey strikes through the heart of Cheshire, serving the salt-fields around Middlewich and Northwich, en route to the Potteries where the prime sponsor of the canal, Josiah Wedgwood, needed reliable transport for his pottery wares. One of the true marvels of the inland waterways system is on this canal at Anderton, where a hydraulic lift lowers boats 50 feet to the River Weaver. Aqueducts, embankments and long tunnels add to the spectacle.

Another industrial lifeline was the Shropshire Union Canal, built in direct competition to the Trent and Mersey as this was seen as a threat to the future of the port of Chester. This canal originally linked Chester and Nantwich, the main towns of the north and south of the county, but it was never a financial success, even when extended towards Wolverhampton in 1835, for by then the railways were in their ascendancy. Branches of this canal reach into Wales and to the hated Trent and Mersey at Middlewich.

The Peak Forest Canal, in north-east Cheshire, was conceived in the 1790s as an outlet for vast limestone quarries in the hills above Buxton. It was the last link in an inventive network of tramways, inclined railways and waterways that brought this vital raw material to the industries and docks of the Manchester basin. The Macclesfield Canal, which joins with the Peak Forest, was an outlet for the coal, stone and cloth of the Pennine foothill communities.

The walks in this book explore aspects of all these features, unveiling faces of Cheshire that even locals may find refreshing and surprising.

Oak Cottages, Styal

1 Redesmere and Capesthorne

This is an ideal introduction to walking in lowland Cheshire. From a renowned mere with a wealth of bird life, it passes through the landscaped estate surrounding the imposing Capesthorne Hall. The return stretch to the mere is via rich, dairy-cattle pasture, pheasant-rearing country and woodland vivid with bluebells in late spring.

START Redesmere, off A34 between Congleton and Alderley Edge

DISTANCE 2¾ miles (4.4km)

TIME 1½ hours

PARKING Free, beside Redesmere

ROUTE FEATURES Woodland, waterside & field paths; two busy main road crossings; c. 22 stiles.

🥾 Put the mere on your left and walk along the lane. Take the waymarked stile on the left about 200 yds after leaving the water, and follow the path across the meadow to another stile onto a path beside woods. At the end bear left along the bridleway through the woodland edge to join a roughly surfaced track near to Redesmere Sailing Club **A**.

The mere was once renowned for its floating island, an immense mat of reeds that meandered with the wind across the water; this is now firmly anchored to the bank. About 50 yds before a gate across the track take the footpath, left, to a footbridge, beyond which trace the sandy path through the trees at the head of the mere.

🏁 An information board at the southwest corner of the mere features some of the more common water birds you're likely to see here. Some of these, like the **swans**, **Canada geese** and **mallard** you just can't miss, but others such as **pochard** are more elusive. Keep an eye out, too, for **buzzards** during your walk.

PUBLIC TRANSPORT None

REFRESHMENTS Ice-cream van on-site most days, otherwise pub and village farm shop at Marton, 2½ miles south

PUBLIC TOILETS None

ORDNANCE SURVEY MAPS Explorer 268 (Wilmslow, Macclesfield & Congleton)

Capesthorne Hall and lake

Carefully cross the main road to the stile virtually opposite. This field-edge path soon reaches the edge of an ornamental lake smothered, in summer, with yellow water lilies. Keep left to another stile and then reclaim the waterside path as the imposing Capesthorne Hall comes into view beyond another lake.

B Cross over the old driveway (not the bridge) and walk beyond the lake to a stile into an access road. At the end cross the lane and take the footpath opposite, heading half-left to a stile. Beyond, follow the direction indicated by the arrow. Cross the farm road to a stile beside a gate, then another beyond a concrete water butt (beware the plank bridge at this stile). Turn left along the field edge and follow this right around (ignore the stile into woodland) to a stile beyond a gate.

Two more waymarked stiles take you to a dirt lane. Turn left, take the bend and fork left to and through a stile, then head for the left of the barns. Take two stiles into the farmyard edge and walk along the driveway left of the buildings. Immediately past the hedge turn left along the rough lane **C**. Pass by the thatched cottage and pick up a path into the bluebell woods soon afterwards.

Turn left at the junction beneath enormous oaks, soon joining a rough lane to gain the main road. Turn right along the footpath, then in 250 yds turn left along Fanshawe Lane back to Redesmere.

Capesthorne Hall is one of Cheshire's greatest houses, home to the Bromley Davenport family since Norman times. The current building dates from 1719, with later, Victorian embellishments. While the house itself can be visited, the main attractions for many are the fine rose gardens and arboretum. Open April to October, Wednesdays, Sundays and Bank Holidays.

? *How many species of birds are illustrated on the board?*

GPS WAYPOINTS

🖊	SJ 848 713	**B**	SJ 840 725
A	SJ 848 718	**C**	SJ 835 716

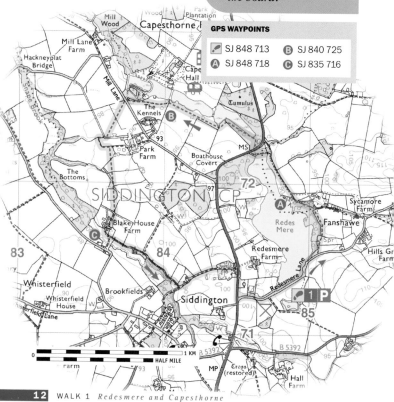

Lymm

START Lymm

DISTANCE 2¼ miles (3.6km)

TIME 1–1½ hours

PARKING Free at Lymm library/market

ROUTE FEATURES Wooded valley, waterside paths; village lanes; ideal for dogs on leads

This short, easy walk explores the heart of Lymm village before joining a waterside path around the scenic and peaceful Lymm Dam lake, an excellent place for bird watching and fishing. Along the way is the earliest canal in England, busy with colourful narrowboats for much of the year.

🥾 From the car park take the path beside the canal (left) and turn right down the cobbled lane past The Saddlers Arms. Keep ahead and turn left along Eagle Brow. Turn right just before the millpond along the narrow 'The Dingle', which becomes a surfaced path up this wooded chasm known as Slitten Gorge. The pond once powered a slitting mill that cut strips of iron used in the manufacture of nails, hoops and horseshoes. Remain with the path to reach steps up to the A56 road.

🅐 Cross directly over, picking up the path for The Bongs. This runs above the bank of the lake known

Slitting mill pond

PUBLIC TRANSPORT Buses to Lymm from Warrington and Altrincham

REFRESHMENTS Cafés, pubs and tearooms in Lymm

PUBLIC TOILETS Lymm

ORDNANCE SURVEY MAPS Explorer 276 (Bolton, Wigan & Warrington)

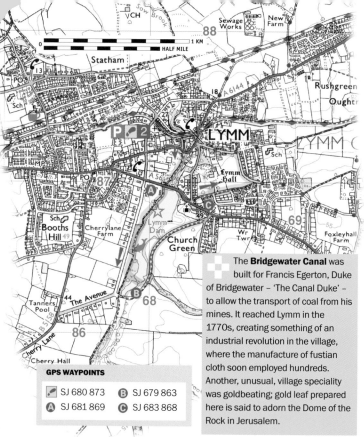

GPS WAYPOINTS

| 📍 SJ 680 873 | **B** SJ 679 863 |
| **A** SJ 681 869 | **C** SJ 683 868 |

> The **Bridgewater Canal** was built for Francis Egerton, Duke of Bridgewater – 'The Canal Duke' – to allow the transport of coal from his mines. It reached Lymm in the 1770s, creating something of an industrial revolution in the village, where the manufacture of fustian cloth soon employed hundreds. Another, unusual, village speciality was goldbeating; gold leaf prepared here is said to adorn the Dome of the Rock in Jerusalem.

as Lymm Dam, created from the village marsh when the turnpike road was routed across a new dam in 1821. The lake is teeming with water birds, including herons and great crested grebes. Keep an eye out for the colourful flashes of dragonflies.

Follow the path to and past a wooden bench. In less than 100 yds, fork left into the grove of magnificent beeches to find steps and a bridge across a brook. Cross this and turn immediately left along the path beneath the gnarled roots of a beech. This brings you to an iron footbridge across a narrow neck of the lake and a wooden one soon afterwards.

B Turn left off this along a waterside path that gradually climbs up from the lake. Keep left

Bridgewater Canal

at any forks, pausing to enjoy these superb woodlands that were partially replanted in the early 1900s on the orders of the wealthy industrialist, Lord Leverhulme.

Pass by a bench beneath enormous beeches above an arm of the lake, to reach a wide grassy area. Follow the sandy path across this to reach a car park. Go through this and bear left to the main road. Turn left to find St Mary's Church, a Victorian building on an originally Saxon site.

C Carefully cross the main road from the church car park, looking for a tarred path from the back of the small triangular green opposite.

Follow this through to an estate road and go along this. At the corner take the narrow snicket on the left, then turn right along the enclosed path. At the footpath post take the steps, left, and turn left along the sunken lane.

At the very end turn left along the road that soon becomes cobbled, falling to the village cross and stocks. Turn right, pass by the Golden Fleece and then take the canalside path, left, back to the car park.

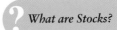

? *What are Stocks?*

3 *Higher Poynton*

START Nelson Pit Visitor Centre, Higher Poynton
DISTANCE 2½ miles (4km)
TIME 1½ hours
PARKING Free, at start
ROUTE FEATURES Easy walking on canal towpath; rough lanes; byroads and field paths. c. 10 stiles. Dogs will need lifting over some stiles, and kept on leads in pastureland

This easy, largely level walk follows the towpath of the Macclesfield Canal through low foothills at the edge of the Peak District. It then joins the track-beds of former colliery tramroads and railways that once served the long-gone coalfield here. Along the way are flower-rich woodlands and verdant pastureland in a tranquil area with distant views to the moors.

Walk through the upper car park onto the towpath of the Macclesfield Canal. Turn left and follow the waterway away from the busy boatyard and beneath bridge 14.

A Beyond the small wood, take the stile beside the fingerpost on your left, signed for Prince's Incline and Middlewood Way. This is the route of one of the old tramroads in the area. In the woods are the remains of the former Canal Pit.

The canal was opened in 1831, making it one of the last to be built in England. The wharf here at **Higher Poynton** exported coal from dozens of the small pits in the compact coalfield. As well as coal, the canal carried silk and cotton from the mills of Congleton, Macclesfield and Bollington, and building stone. One unusual cargo was manure. Before city sewers were built, human waste, called 'night soil', was collected at depots in Manchester where it was processed before being sold to farmers for £3 per ton. It was an excellent fertiliser.

PUBLIC TRANSPORT Regular daily (not Sundays or BH) bus 391 from Stockport to start (Boars Head pub)
REFRESHMENTS Pub and coffee shop at start
PUBLIC TOILETS At start, including disabled access toilet
ORDNANCE SURVEY MAPS Explorer 268 (Wilmslow, Macclesfield & Congleton)

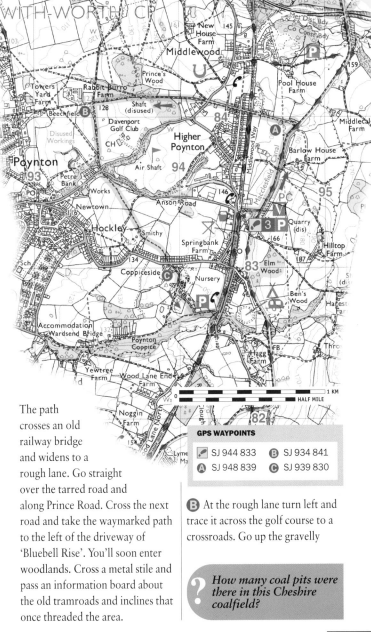

The path crosses an old railway bridge and widens to a rough lane. Go straight over the tarred road and along Prince Road. Cross the next road and take the waymarked path to the left of the driveway of 'Bluebell Rise'. You'll soon enter woodlands. Cross a metal stile and pass an information board about the old tramroads and inclines that once threaded the area.

GPS WAYPOINTS

✎ SJ 944 833		**B**	SJ 934 841
A SJ 948 839		**C**	SJ 939 830

B At the rough lane turn left and trace it across the golf course to a crossroads. Go up the gravelly

? *How many coal pits were there in this Cheshire coalfield?*

track opposite, to the right of Anson Road. Climb the stile and pass right of the stables, then up-paddock to a kissing-gate. Pass the shattered oak and head for the top-right corner kissing-gate. Use this and then the stile on the left in 30 paces; then head half-right to a hidden waymarked stile in trees. Go straight ahead (not right) to another stile in a corner, then across the pasture to a stile into a wide gap between houses.

C Cross the road and take the rough lane for the kennels. Keep left and follow this past the kennels and the bungalow, 'Hillcrest', to reach steps and a kissing gate. Go

The **Visitor Centre** (open daily, 10.00–16.00) is built on the site of the former Nelson Coal Pit. This has a wealth of information about the coalfield and the canal and railways that took away the coal. At the entrance to the car park is a steel sculpture. A plaque attached to the plinth shows the distribution of the former collieries.

left and follow the upper path above Poynton Coppice. At the car park turn left along the old railway, now the Middlewood Way, to reach the former Higher Poynton Station. The inclined path, left, leads to The Boar's Head; the Visitor Centre is then over the bridge. ●

The Macclesfield Canal at Anson Wharf

Alderley Edge

Countless paths thread the wooded Edge above Alderley. Today the National Trust owns and manages the area, which is famed for its old copper mines, specimen trees and flocks of birds. This easy walk offers a glimpse of these, and fine views to the high hills of the Peak District.

START National Trust Car Park, The Wizard

DISTANCE $2\frac{1}{2}$ miles (4km)

TIME $1\frac{1}{2}$ hours

PARKING Pay and Display; note the closing time shown at the entrance

ROUTE FEATURES Woodland and heathland paths; there are sudden sharp drops, so children should be strictly supervised; one main road crossing at awkward location

4

From the car park, slip left of the shelter to reach the nearby track. The Wizard Inn is left; ahead is a NT Information Centre (opening restricted), which has displays telling the long history of The Edge and details of any trips down the old mines.

Turn right, pass the barrier and walk the woodland-edge track, revealing fine views across to the peak of Shutlingsloe. The track sweeps left, shortly passing the first of the old mining remains, Engine Vein on your left. Remain with the track to reach a gate at a sharp-right bend. Use the hand-gate, left and walk straight ahead, shortly reaching the rocky viewpoint at Stormy Point **A**. As you reach this open area, note the two paths off to your left by pines; your way

The **copper mines of Alderley** were certainly worked in Roman times, and are the oldest recorded mines in England, nearly 2,000 years old. The remains visible today date from the 19th century. In one of the old mines, the mythical Wizard of Alderley is said to guard 40 knights on white horses, waiting to come to England's rescue in time of war!

PUBLIC TRANSPORT None

REFRESHMENTS Wizard Inn and weekend tearooms at start

PUBLIC TOILETS At start, including disabled access toilet

ORDNANCE SURVEY MAPS Explorer 268 (Wilmslow, Macclesfield & Congleton)

onwards is the second of these. Take a breather to enjoy the huge views across to the Dark Peak and Kinder Scout.

Return to the second path (waymarked) noted earlier, which drops steadily down to cross a seasonal brook on a little flat bridge. Ignore the main path right; instead go ahead up the slope, slipping ahead off a bend to reach the block of concrete in the trees ahead, marking the site of an Armada Beacon.

> **?** *Who provided the plaque at the beacon?*

Put the wall on your left and walk the uppermost path to reach Castle Rock, the most famous viewpoint here *(beware – steep drops)*, with great views across north east

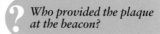

GPS WAYPOINTS

✏ SJ 859 772	**C** SJ 852 774
A SJ 860 778	**D** SJ 857 775
B SJ 855 778	

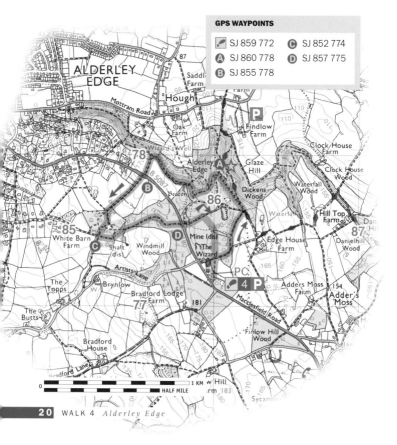

North-east Cheshire from Stormy Point

Cheshire. Leave along the path around the outside of the fenced pasture to reach the road at an awkward crossing.

B Cross carefully and take the waymarked path beside the fence to a stile, then past gnarled oaks and into the woodland edge. At a wider track near a gate turn left. This track soon drifts right and passes through an area of ponds, gorse and broom. In about 350 yds there is a wide crossing path at right angles, just before the main path starts to descend. Turn left here **C** and keep ahead, roughly along the left margin of the heath.

Take the main path into the woods, soon reaching a National Trust sign. Pass right of this, then go left at a fork to reach old workings at a clearing in the woods. Head half right on the continuing wide path up to the road.

D Cross this and go back into the woods beside the house. Go straight ahead along the widest, sunken path to a waymarked cross-path in 150 yds. Turn right along this compacted-surface path to return to the start. ●

5 Styal and Quarry Bank Mill

One of Britain's finest planned industrial communities, the sublime Quarry Bank Mill and associated workers' housing, lies at the heart of a massive National Trust owned country park just 10 miles south of Manchester city centre. This easy walk makes the most of this heritage, and of the superb wooded gorge of the River Bollin.

START Twinnies Bridge car park, Wilmslow

DISTANCE 2½ miles (4km)

TIME 1½ hours (plus time at the Mill, allow at least 1½ hours more)

PARKING Free car park at Twinnies Bridge. (If Twinnies car park is full, there is car parking [charge] at Quarry Bank Mill itself.)

ROUTE FEATURES Field, woodland and village paths; dogs on leads only

Park at Twinnies Bridge and take the path beside the toilet block, keeping right at the fork to reach a footbridge over the Bollin. Cross this and fork right within a few paces, before reaching an information board. At the kissing-gate turn left and take the path through the hay meadows.

A Keep to the upper path, climb the stile and follow the initially cobbled path through a green tunnel of undergrowth to a fieldside path. Keep ahead, through a gate, then two kissing-gates, to join a surfaced path beside a car park above the Mill.

Pass by the bus shelter (*bus-users start/finish here*) and go down the narrow path to a driveway. Turn right and then go left in 100 yds, just before the drive to the Apprentice House. Follow this path across pastures towards the distant village. At the gate turn right along the rough lane to reach the Methodist Chapel here in Styal village.

PUBLIC TRANSPORT Bus 200 from Manchester Airport and Wilmslow every day to Quarry Bank Mill

REFRESHMENTS Tearoom and restaurant at the Mill. Pub and shop in Styal village

PUBLIC TOILETS At start (weekends only), at Mill during opening hours, including disabled access toilet

ORDNANCE SURVEY MAPS Explorer 268 (Wilmslow, Macclesfield & Congleton)

B Take the sandy path in front of the lovely Farm Fold Cottages to the village cross; here turn right up the cobbled lane. This brings you to the former village shop, later a co-operative, and beyond this the sublime houses and terraces of Oak Cottages.

Return to the cross and turn right to pass Norcliffe Chapel, entering woods beyond an information board. Keep right at the fork, falling to cross Chapel Bridge.

Styal was a rural hamlet until an Irish businessman, Samuel Greg, established a water-powered cotton-spinning mill here beside the River Bollin. The business boomed, and Greg was forced to adapt village barns and build cottages to house his rapidly expanding workforce. His workers included children rescued from poorhouses and orphanages in Manchester; they were housed in the Apprentice House and given schooling and fair meals as well as working in the mill. Greg, who realised, as did Robert Owen in New Lanark and Richard Arkwright in Cromford, that the better the workers were treated, the more productive they became, also provided social and educational facilities for adults. The entire village and Mill passed to the National Trust in 1939, the gift of the last of the Gregs.

GPS WAYPOINTS

🖉	SJ 839 822	**C**	SJ 831 832
A	SJ 838 823	**D**	SJ 835 829
B	SJ 836 835		

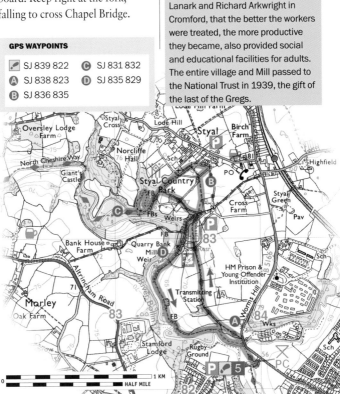

Keep left beyond; an undulating path through superb beech and exotic tree woodlands reaches Kingfisher Bridge . Cross this, bear left up steps and follow a wide path to reach a junction by an information board. Turn right, and keep ahead across the rough road to reach the driveway down to Quarry Bank Mill.

The Mill itself is fascinating and repays an extended visit; original steam and water-powered machinery now produces calico for National Trust garments and souvenirs.

D To return to Twinnies Bridge take the sandy path from the far end of the mill yard past the Mill Kitchen. Stick with this, keeping left at two junctions to cross Heron's Pool Bridge. Keep left, then go right along a riverside path back to the footbridge near the car park and to the starting point of the walk.

> **?** *In which year did Samuel Greg establish the mill?*

Quarry Bank Mill

Forest Chapel

START	Standing Stone Car Park
DISTANCE	2½ miles (4km)
TIME	1½ hours
PARKING	Free car park
ROUTE FEATURES	Woodland and field paths; back lanes and farm tracks. c. 10 stiles; dogs not encouraged. Short, steep climb at the end

From a car park hidden along narrow lanes, this easy walk first plunges into the woodlands of Macclesfield Forest, high above the Cheshire Plain. Rising to a secluded hamlet in folds of the hills, it then drops down to the peaceful valley of Tor Brook, with a handy pub, before picking up a streamside path amid hay meadows and below superb, rolling moorland.

From the bottom right of the car park pass the barrier and then turn right along the wide grassy swathe. Off to the right, felling has opened out tantalising views across to the high moors and the Cat and Fiddle Inn. Cresting a low rise, the path descends to a fingerpost for Trentabank at the edge of the forest.

Turn left along the gravel path into woodland. As it winds through the

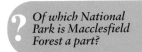
? *Of which National Park is Macclesfield Forest a part?*

The Forest Chapel

PUBLIC TRANSPORT Infrequent buses to The Stanley Arms
REFRESHMENTS The Stanley Arms (200 yds off route)
PUBLIC TOILETS None
ORDNANCE SURVEY MAPS Explorer OL24 (The Peak District – White Peak area)

trees keep an eye out for wildflowers, particularly in areas where tree cover has been thinned; in spring wood sorrel and anemones, in summer foxgloves.

Macclesfield Forest was established last century on 1,000 acres of upland sheep pastures. There are red deer here, but you'll be lucky to see one. Wild birds abound; listen for the high-pitched pipping of the goldcrest, Britain's smallest bird, high in the pine, spruce and larch.

Steps drop to a long stretch of boardwalk crossing the boggy source of the River Bollin; a dry path continues beyond to a fingerpost for Forest Chapel. Turn right up to a lane, along which turn right. Remain with it to reach Forest Chapel.

Ⓐ Take the rough lane to the right of the church (vehicles prohibited sign). This, Oven Lane, gradually drops into the valley of Tor Brook. Superb views stretch ahead to rolling moors and south to the peak of Shutlingsloe. At the lane foot turn left, then left again at the junction. Your route is shortly right, along the driveway to Chambers Farm; The Stanley Arms pub is 200 yds farther up the lane.

Ⓑ Go through the farmyard and the tiny walker's gate, turn left behind the barn to a waymarked

Wildboar Clough from Standing Stone

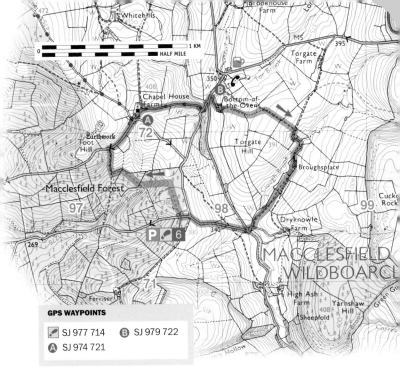

GPS WAYPOINTS

🖉 SJ 977 714   **B** SJ 979 722

A SJ 974 721

gate, then another leading into pasture. Follow the sunken path beside a wall to a ladder-stile. Climb this and look half-left for another, once over which turn right beside the wall to reach a stone stile.

Go ahead down into the ravine, looking slightly right for a stile. Turn right and trace this old field road past a fingerpost and above Clough Brook for 150 yds to a narrow, railed footbridge. Rise up to Broughsplace Farm.

Follow the access road and bear right to the minor road. Turn left; then right, climbing back to the car park. ●

Forest Chapel hamlet huddles around a little stone church first built in 1673, possibly on a much older site. It is one of the highest in England, and retains the medieval custom of rush bearing. Each summer (first Sunday after August 12th) a service of renewal is held; in older times this was when a fresh layer of sweet-smelling rushes was spread over the earth floor of the chapel. Today, sheaves of rushes decorate the church.

7 *Wybunbury Moss*

START Wybunbury
DISTANCE 2½ miles (4km)
TIME 1½ hours
PARKING Free village car park along gravelled drive near the new St Chad's Church. Note closing time stated at the gate
ROUTE FEATURES Village paths; field paths; farm lanes; suitable for agile dogs; c. 15 stiles and gates

The eye-catching tower of Wybunbury's now demolished old church is Cheshire's equivalent of the famous leaning tower of Pisa, although not at the same angle. This walk is an easy circuit of the old Cheshire village, dropping gently to a track around the remarkable Wybunbury Moss, one of Britain's rarest natural habitats.

Return to the village's Main Street and turn right. Just beyond the Post Office turn left along Kiln Lane and walk to the end. Take the waymarked stile half-left and follow the path across two stiles to enter manicured grounds. Trace the hedge to the gravelled drive. Go straight over to find a fingerpost pointing left along a high-hedged path.

Continue along a wide green swathe behind bungalows to reach an old farm lane. Turn right down this, immediately reaching the boundary of Wybunbury Moss.

Ⓐ The old lane skirts the Moss. To the right, the lean of the distant church tower is distinctly visible on its low ridge. Pass behind the cottage and remain with the grassy path to reach a tarred lane. Keep ahead past several houses; as it bends sharp left, fork right to a stile beside a gate, regaining a path along the top of rough pasture above the Moss. At the far end, take the short track between gates beneath tall alders and then turn right over the stile. Climb a further stile into the edge of the Moss and walk ahead towards the distant St Chad's church tower.

PUBLIC TRANSPORT Buses to Wybunbury from Crewe
REFRESHMENTS Pub and shop in Wybunbury
PUBLIC TOILETS None
ORDNANCE SURVEY MAPS Explorer 257 (Crewe & Nantwich)

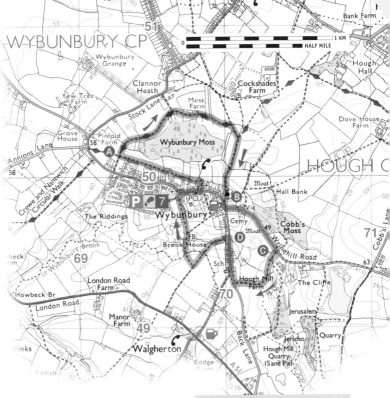

Keep left beyond the boardwalk to cross a flat concrete bridge, continuing ahead up to the hand-gate into the churchyard. Climb to another gate virtually beneath the tower. The tower, all that survives of the fifth church built on this site, is about four feet out-of-true.

> **When was the last service held at the old church?**

B Keep straight ahead past the tower down to the road opposite

GPS WAYPOINTS

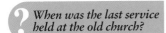 SJ 696 498		**C** SJ 703 495
A SJ 692 502		**D** SJ 700 495
B SJ 700 498		

the old Red Lion Inn (N.B. not The Swan). Turn sharp left along Wrinehill Road and walk to a sub-station on your right.

C Here, turn right along the farm lane, cross the bridge and walk to the bend. Turn right to a higher stile into a thicket; walk up through this to another stile and turn right along the field edge. A further stile leads to a short, brambly stretch and a gate into a lane. Turn right, then keep right at the school to find Sally Clarkes Lane, along which turn left.

D Immediately over a cattle-grid, turn left on the fieldside path to a stile up steps. Turn right to cross another stile; then left beside the hedge for 150 yds. Turn back right on the signed cross-field path to a stile, dropping then to a track. Take the path opposite down to a footbridge; then go straight up the field (not half-right) to a kissing-gate. Turn left into the sports ground to find the car park. ●

This tranquil area of birch woods, reeds and pines is one of only two spots in Britain where such a floating bog exists, and is protected as a **National Nature Reserve**. The skin of peaty vegetation is barely a yard thick, beneath which is a water-filled hollow up to 40 feet deep, caused by the subsidence of the rocks below. The area is rich in rare plants and insects, and is a haven for all sorts of wildlife.

Wybunbury's old church, from the Moss

Beeston Castle and the Peckforton Hills

8

START Beeston Castle
DISTANCE 3 miles (4.8km)
TIME 1½–2 hours
PARKING Beeston Castle. Free for castle visitors, otherwise Pay and Display. Car park closes at time posted on gate
ROUTE FEATURES One short, moderately steep climb, otherwise easy walking on lanes, and paths. c. 10 stiles. Suitable for dogs on leads

This walk explores a section of Cheshire's Sandstone Trail, a route following the spine of the county from north to south. From the spectacular site of Beeston Castle, footpaths meander into the Peckforton Hills, a wooded ridge rising high enough to unveil views to north Wales and concealing a remarkable Victorian Gothic castle, now a hotel.

The gatehouse of Beeston Castle beckons opposite the car park, but save this treat for the end of the walk. Instead, turn left along the lane and then take the path to the right beside a Sandstone Trail information board. Trace the wall until it curves away, at which point keep half-left with the waymark along a woodland path. Follow this down through the pines to a lane.

A A kissing-gate up steps left of the driveway leads to a footbridge in a wooded hollow. Continue ahead along the fieldside path towards the woods. The round keep and towers of the Gothic Peckforton Castle (built in the 1840s for the Tollemache family at a cost of £67,847.9s.7½d) peek out above the trees while behind you, the remarkable site of Beeston Castle is revealed.

PUBLIC TRANSPORT None
REFRESHMENTS Café and snacks at Beeston Castle; country pubs within 1 mile of start
PUBLIC TOILETS For castle visitors
ORDNANCE SURVEY MAPS Explorer 257 (Crewe & Nantwich)

Beeston Castle rises above a 'magpie manor'

The Romans originally occupied the site of **Beeston Castle**. Today's remarkable ruins are of the fortress built in 1337 by Ranulf, Earl of Chester; the well here is 360 feet (110m) deep. The commanding views from the top allowed the medieval Marcher Lords to help stop incursions by Welsh raiders. The castle is open every day except around Christmas.

This fieldside path emerges into a lane; turn right to a track on the left in 400 yds, a Peckforton Estate access and also the Sandstone Trail. This skirts the foot of the steep, wooded slopes of the Peckforton Hills, oak woods vibrant with birdsong; listen for jays, green woodpeckers and warblers. Squirrels abound, as do pheasants when released from nearby rearing pens. Way off to your right are the mountains of Flintshire; can you also pick out the cathedral towers at Chester and Liverpool?

B At the major crossing of paths and tracks at a clearing turn left, soon picking up a long series of steps that climb to a gap through the sandstone ridge. At the top turn left; then in 50 paces go right to follow the sometimes muddy path down through the woods to meet a tarred drive. Turn right to pass beneath the arched gatehouse of Peckforton Castle and onto a lane.

C Look half-right for a well-hidden stile, and head half-left across the huge field towards the distant woods. Take the stile into these woods; a well-trodden path leads to another stile at the far side. Climb this and keep left beside a pond. Sight the large silage-clamp (secured by numerous car tyres) and head for this. Take the right-hand stile by a field gate, cross the muddy farm lane to another stile (not the footbridge) and follow the track to a road. Turn left to a junction; from here follow the signs back to Beeston Castle.

GPS WAYPOINTS

🖊 SJ 540 590	Ⓑ SJ 528 575
Ⓐ SJ 538 588	Ⓒ SJ 538 575

? *Which organisation manages Beeston Castle?*

9 Marbury and the Anderton Lift

START Marbury Country Park

DISTANCE 3½ miles (5.6km)

TIME 2 hours

PARKING Pay and display

OPEN 09.00–20.00 May–Sept, 09.00–17.00 Oct–April

ROUTE FEATURES Level walking on good paths, canal towpath and minor roads. c. 12 stiles

Cheshire is famed for its meres, large, often shallow lakes with a wealth of bird life. This easy walk visits one of the most renowned, before a short cross-country stroll is rewarded by a close encounter with one of the true marvels of the canal network. The return leg is through woodland containing many unusual and specimen trees.

 Make sure you take binoculars. Walk to the countryside rangers' office and, with this to your left, go along the drive and turn left at the junction towards the bird hide.

The terrace you're on is one of the few remaining structures of a vast country estate that dates back to AD1216. It had a chequered history (told on a display at the far end of the car park). The immense Victorian country house here was demolished in 1969; the Country Park was established in 1975. The arboretum is well worth exploring.

Divert down the steps on the right to the bird hide at the edge of Budworth Mere. This is one of the best places to watch water birds (and others) in the north-west of England. Rarities seen include bittern, and red kite straying from their stronghold in mid-Wales.

Return to the terrace and turn right, tracing the drive around to the main road. Turn right and cross to a kissing-gate beyond the old bus shelter. Use this and walk ahead, with a hedge on your right. The path drops into a wooded dingle, crosses a footbridge and

PUBLIC TRANSPORT Infrequent bus services to Marbury and Anderton

REFRESHMENTS Pub, shop and tearooms along the way

PUBLIC TOILETS At start, including disabled access toilet

ORDNANCE SURVEY MAPS Explorer 267 (Northwich & Delamere Forest)

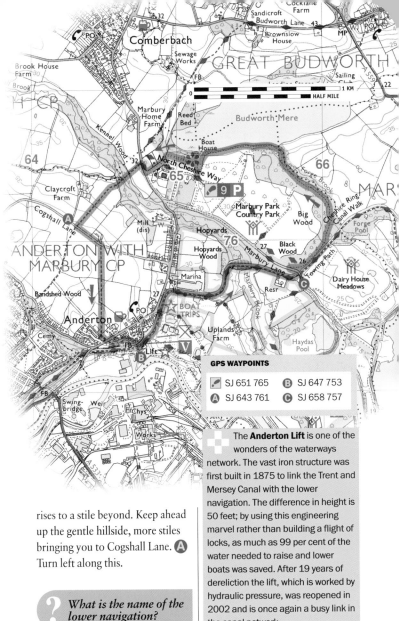

GPS WAYPOINTS

✏️ SJ 651 765		🅑 SJ 647 753
🅐 SJ 643 761		🅒 SJ 658 757

rises to a stile beyond. Keep ahead up the gentle hillside, more stiles bringing you to Cogshall Lane. 🅐 Turn left along this.

? *What is the name of the lower navigation?*

The **Anderton Lift** is one of the wonders of the waterways network. The vast iron structure was first built in 1875 to link the Trent and Mersey Canal with the lower navigation. The difference in height is 50 feet; by using this engineering marvel rather than building a flight of locks, as much as 99 per cent of the water needed to raise and lower boats was saved. After 19 years of dereliction the lift, which is worked by hydraulic pressure, was reopened in 2002 and is once again a busy link in the canal network.

Take the stile on the right opposite the lone house. At the far side of this field turn left along the hedge-line to find a stile and sleeper-bridge near a wooden pylon. Cross these and go ahead to another stile at a corner, then three others (all waymarked). From these fields are fine views east (left) to the line of the Peak District hills.

At the extreme far side turn left alongside the fence, take the gap by a gate and walk to the road. Turn left; then right along the lane to the Stanley Arms. Not far past this take the footbridge across the canal and keep the water to your left. In a short distance turn right to find the Canal Exhibition Centre. The exhibition here is well worth spending some time at. Boat trips are available (tel. 01606 786777).

🅑 Return to the canal towpath and turn right. Stick with this for about a mile, briefly leaving it to cross a canal arm leading to a boatyard. Soon after passing beneath pipelines, leave the towpath at a concrete bridge 🅒, cross this and take the footpath, right, for Big Wood. Keep right at any junctions in the woods to find a wide, sandy path, along which turn right. This comes close to the canal again before veering off into Big Wood.

Keep left at a fork near massive sycamore and beech trees (staying well above a stream), then right at a fingerpost for 'Mere and Car Park'. Pass by a pond on your left, then fork right to a mereside path, following this all the way back to the car park. ●

The Anderton Lift disgorging its cargo

The Gowy Valley

START Waverton
DISTANCE 4½ miles (7.2km)
TIME 2½ hours
PARKING Eggbridge Lane car park, canalside (free)
ROUTE FEATURES Easy walking on lanes; field paths and towpath; suitable for agile dogs

This walk threads through dimpled countryside to the astonishing Roman Bridges over the River Gowy, a string of medieval packhorse bridges along this ancient trade route between the once thriving port of Chester and the Midlands. Much of this trade passed to the Ellesmere & Chester Canal, opened in 1779; now the Shropshire Union Canal, it is a peaceful end to the walk.

Turn right from the car park, cross the canal and walk on to find Brown Heath Road on your left in 300 yds. Turn up this; just past the speed de-restriction sign, turn right on the shaded driveway to 'Dolly Peg' – there's a fingerpost here. Enter the yard and look carefully immediately past the house for a stile on the left. A narrow fenced path winds beside pasture to a plank footbridge and a kissing-gate. From here a series of four such gates takes the path directly across fields (roughly in line with the radio masts on the ridge) to a hedge gap right of an electricity pylon. Go through the gap then half-left across the pasture to a stile beside an oak. Turn right down the lane.

Keep ahead off the sharp bend on the lesser lane: then straight on as the driveway to Cotton Farm branches right. Beyond bollards the lane becomes a track through marshy woods, shortly reaching the memorable trio of packhorse bridges across the River Gowy here at Hockenhull Platts. Take time to enjoy this peaceful spot, believed

PUBLIC TRANSPORT Buses to Waverton from Chester
REFRESHMENTS Walk Mill café beside the Gowy
PUBLIC TOILETS None
ORDNANCE SURVEY MAPS Explorers 266 (Wirral & Chester) and 267 (Northwich & Delamere Forest)

Hockenhull's **cobbled packhorse bridges** are known as the Roman Bridges. They are not Roman, but lie on the presumed route of the Roman Road between Chester and Nantwich. They probably date from the 1400s, built to allow trains of packhorses to carry salt, cloth and minerals across this marshy terrain. Legend has it, they are haunted by the ghost of a servant girl, Grace Trigg from nearby Hockenhull Hall, who was murdered here by Parliamentarian soldiers during the Civil War in the 1640s.

to be home to otters and with a wealth of other wildlife.

A Head upstream from the middle bridge, river on your left, along a concessionary path from the Reserve to a high footbridge. Cross this and head half-right across the pasture to a lone thorn

Hockenhull Bridge

bush and a field gate, beyond which walk to the stile at the road bridge.

B Cross the bridge and, at the bend in 100 yds, go left at the waymark post. Cross the field in line with the chimney breaking the skyline. You'll reach the Gowy at an imposing new watermill, built on the foundations of a medieval cornmill. Corn is once again ground here at Walk Mill; enjoy a tour and then indulge in the freshest baking at the café here (closed Mondays except BH). Depart along the access road and walk to the right-hand bend in 100 yds. Leave the road and go ahead on the stony fieldside track, shortly passing beneath cables. Just after this, at a fork marked by a decrepit fingerpost, keep right on the path along the right-edge of the copse. At the far end take the stile on the right (not straight on) and trace the left side of this field to the next corner. Turn left over two adjacent stiles, putting a hedge on your right. A couple of pastures bring you to a stile into a track; go left to the road.

C Turn right. Just around the right-bend, enter the field on your left at a wide hedge gap (old fingerpost for Waverton nearby). Keep ahead across the waist of the next three fields, passing just left of the old wind-pump and to the right of a pond, presently reaching a wooded corner. Carry on, woods on your right. Just past the woods, slip half-right into a high-hedged path, following this old track to a canal bridge. Join the towpath, water to your right, and walk back to the start.

GPS WAYPOINTS

🖉 SJ 455 642	**B** SJ 482 647
A SJ 476 657	**C** SJ 476 639

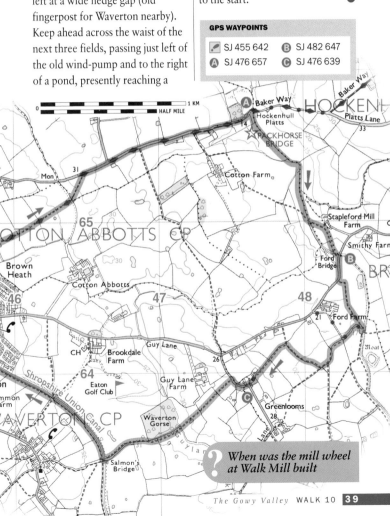

? *When was the mill wheel at Walk Mill built*

11 *Bunbury and the Shroppie*

START Bunbury Church
DISTANCE 4 miles (6.4km)
TIME 2–2½ hours
PARKING Large car parking area immediately east of the church
ROUTE FEATURES Field and canalside paths, back lanes; suitable for agile dogs. c. 12 stiles

Nestling beside the tiny River Gowy, Bunbury is dominated by the wonderful old church of St Boniface. The walk links this to the village's old canal warehouses via a tiny watermill beside a tranquil millpond. Hard to imagine, today, that the church was half-destroyed during the Second World War, and some of the village cottages flattened by bombs.

Bunbury's dispersed village originated as a hamlet huddled round a fortified place (the bury element of the name) where a church was built in Saxon times. Charred timbers found beneath today's church are thought to be the remains of such.

Climb the stile at the bottom end of the car parking area and walk straight downhill to another stile into the car park at Bunbury Mill. This tiny building, virtually built into the dam holding back the millpond, is the latest of a long series to occupy the site since the first one in medieval times. It is open on Sundays and Bank Holiday afternoons between April and September.

Ⓐ Follow Mill Lane back from the millpond to reach a minor road, along which turn right. Stay

Take time to explore **Bunbury**'s magnificent church. There's a superb effigy tomb to Sir Hugh Calveley, a 14th-century knight and another to Sir George Beeston who, in 1588, commanded the ship *Dreadnought* against the Spanish Armada when aged 89. (If locked, the church key is available nearby.)

PUBLIC TRANSPORT Limited bus service to Bunbury
REFRESHMENTS Pubs and shops in Bunbury, café and snacks at canal locks
PUBLIC TOILETS None
ORDNANCE SURVEY MAPS Explorer 257 (Crewe & Nantwich)

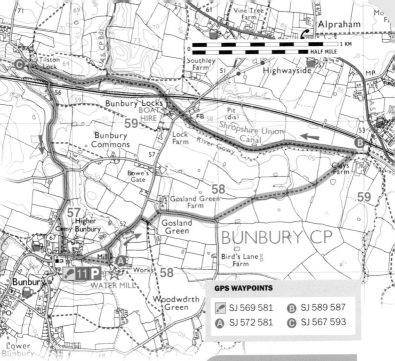

GPS WAYPOINTS

📷 SJ 569 581	Ⓑ SJ 589 587
Ⓐ SJ 572 581	Ⓒ SJ 567 593

with this across the little River Gowy and uphill past typical half-timbered Cheshire cottages. Turn right along the gravelled drive to 'The Barracks' and then look for the stile on the left about 100 yds along this. Go straight over the pasture to a stile beneath a horse chestnut tree, join the lane and turn right.

Remain on this to reach a sharp-right bend. Use the stile on the left here and head a shade right across the field aiming 100 yds right of the tall poplar; behind an ash tree here there is a stiled plank bridge.

❓ *Why is the towpath of the canal so-called?*

Turn right off this alongside the ditch to reach a footbridge and kissing-gate. From this walk in-line to the far side and another kissing-gate near an oak. Drift just left of the line of cables to find the first of three close-knit kissing-gates that lead to the canal towpath.

Ⓑ Turn left. A long, open stretch of canal, offering views across to the Peckforton Hills and Beeston Castle, brings you to the fascinating locks at Bunbury Wharf.

Bunbury and the Shroppie WALK 11 **41**

Staying on the towpath, the character of the canal now changes; this stretch is through damp willow-carr woodland. Beyond the canal the woods are a striking yellow in late spring with yellow flag iris. Off to your left in summer grows the immense giant hogweed. Imported by Victorian plant collectors from south-west Asia, it looks like an enormous cow parsley, the tall white-flowered plant common in hedgerows and ditches. The hogweed, however, is deadly in comparison, as brushing against it can cause serious blisters. It reaches over 10 feet high; admire it from a distance.

C At the next lock leave the canal and turn left past the old mill. Stay on this lane straight over the crossroads. In another 500 yds take the waymarked stile, left, and head towards the houses. On your right here a stile leads to a path through the graveyard and back to the church. ●

The **Shropshire Union Canal** – the 'Shroppie' – opened in 1779. The canalside buildings here are among the finest on the waterway. The long stable buildings are now used for boat building while the old warehouse beside the bridge still has the canal company name painted on its gable wall. Cargo included tons of American maize cake and cotton seed cake, imported through Liverpool Docks and ground at Bunbury Mill. If you have a chance, observe boats negotiating the locks, a short staircase of unusual design that often causes problems.

Eye-catching colour on the Shroppie

Whitegate and the Weaver Navigation

12

START Whitegate

DISTANCE 4½ miles (7.2km)

TIME 2½ hours

PARKING Village green near the church, school and village room

ROUTE FEATURES Easy walking on lanes, field paths and towpath

Some 700 years ago, the largest Cistercian Monastery in England was secluded in the depths of the Cheshire countryside here. This walk drifts past the remaining evidence of this, along the way catching a glimpse of Cheshire's white gold beside a waterway rich in wildlife.

The White Gate was the entrance to the home estate surrounding the abbey founded by Edward I in thanks for deliverance from a storm at sea. The monks were Cistercians, otherwise the White Monks, hence the name. The village church is on the site of the old abbey gate chapel. Join Grange Lane, beside the thatched cottage. In 300 yds fork right on the 'Dead End' lane; past a barrier this becomes a stroll along a secluded dell. Beyond the woods the old lane rises easily amid cornfields. About 300 yds after it levels you'll reach a point where several gates guard field entrances; there's also a fingerpost on the right. Here fork left into the field-edge track and keep ahead in 250 yds when a farm lane joins from the left.

A At the end of the first field turn left through the barrier into a hedge-side grassy track. In 200 yds swap sides, continuing then round a right corner of the field. The hedge becomes a fence; look carefully just before the next corner for a stile, left, into a path, down which turn left. Wind with this through to a solid footbridge and, beyond, a gate into a driveway

PUBLIC TRANSPORT None

REFRESHMENTS None

PUBLIC TOILETS None

ORDNANCE SURVEY MAPS Explorer 267 (Northwich & Delamere Forest)

The Weaver Navigation and Winsford Salt Mine

at one of Cheshire's salt mines, producing salt for the chemical industry and winter roads. Once over the second bridge turn left on the gravelly towpath. For the next mile the path is a delightful ramble beside this tranquil, wildlife-rich waterway, along what Edward I described as 'the fairest vale in all England', naming it Vale Royal.

C At Vale Royal Locks cross the waterway and swing right on the access track. Cross the bridge over the old river before turning left along the gated drive beyond the car park. Remain on this all the way* through to the imposing building at Vale Royal. Continue on the driveway; at housing on your right, cross to the tarred old footpath on the left, following this beneath an imposing avenue of trees back to Whitegate.

at Bradford Mill. Slip to the end of this and turn right along the lane. Cross the bridge below the entrance to a chalet complex and then fork left on the access lane to the canal bridges.

B Cross the bridges over the Weaver Navigation. To your right, the superstructure is the headgear

> The **Weaver Navigation** was created in the 1720s by canalising a stretch of the River Weaver to make transport of salt from the local mines more economic; Josiah Wedgwood also used the cut to move china clay from the sea towards the Potteries. It was hugely expanded in the 1880s to serve the chemical works and complexes at Northwich and onward shipping to the Mersey Estuary near Runcorn. Today it is largely the preserve of pleasure craft.

*(N.B. – if a footpath diversion [summer 2010] is still in place, turn right at the waymark 200 yds before the gateway into the golf course, walk up the dingle, left across the footbridge and ahead on the marked footpath over the golf course. Turn left on the estate road, then back right in 150 yds onto the path beneath the avenue of trees [or continue on the road to see the abbey site].) ●

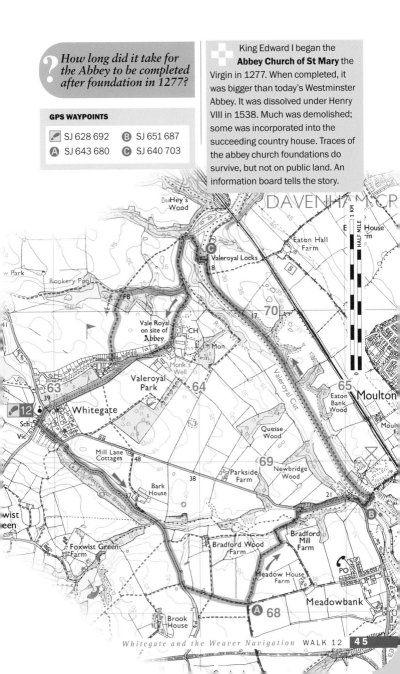

? *How long did it take for the Abbey to be completed after foundation in 1277?*

GPS WAYPOINTS

📷 SJ 628 692   **B** SJ 651 687
A SJ 643 680   **C** SJ 640 703

King Edward I began the **Abbey Church of St Mary** the Virgin in 1277. When completed, it was bigger than today's Westminster Abbey. It was dissolved under Henry VIII in 1538. Much was demolished; some was incorporated into the succeeding country house. Traces of the abbey church foundations do survive, but not on public land. An information board tells the story.

13 *Bel o' th' Hill*

START Bel o' th' Hill

DISTANCE 3½ miles (5.6km)

TIME 2–2½ hours

PARKING Roadside opposite The Blue Bell pub; 3 miles NNW of Whitchurch, signposted off the A41

ROUTE FEATURES Back lanes, towpath and field paths; suitable for dogs (on leads in pastures)

From a gem of a country pub, this easy stroll along quiet back lanes and byways picks up the towpath of the Llangollen Canal as it makes its raised course across the low-lying Willey Moor. The Sandstone Trail is then joined at a secluded pub, rising gently past old cottages and farms to a remote old church lost in the fields.

Facing the pub, bear right to the main road. Cross straight over to join the lane for Willey Moor, and keep ahead. This peaceful lane gradually gains height enough to reveal views right (west) to the hills of Flintshire and left across the rolling patchwork quilt of the rich pasturelands of the Cheshire/Shropshire borderland. Remain with the lane past several houses and Bel o' th' Hill Farm, after which the lane drops into a dip.

Ⓐ At the bottom take the waymarked stile on the left and drift slightly right to pass just right of the smaller pylon. Look along the hedgeline just beyond the gate for a high stile; take this and turn left beside the hedge. A canal overbridge soon comes into view. On reaching this do not cross it but, rather, slip to the left of it onto the towpath and head north, water to your right.

The half-timbered **Blue Bell Inn** is a delight. The hamlet is named after it – the Bell on the Hill. Partially dating from the 14th century, it oozes character, from the quirky little spiral staircase to the tale of the phantom duck walled up in a bottle. Look forward to a visit as you walk this little known area of south Cheshire.

PUBLIC TRANSPORT None

REFRESHMENTS Pubs at start and on route

PUBLIC TOILETS None

ORDNANCE SURVEY MAPS Explorer 257 (Crewe & Nantwich)

This is the Llangollen branch of the Shropshire Union Canal system; its destination is that famous Welsh town some 30 miles away. Few stretches of the waterways network can have so many wildflowers as the stretch now followed. The blooms in July and August are magnificent, an artist's palette of natural colours; purple and white loosestrife, meadowsweet, willowherb, woundwort, vetches and trefoils present a marvellous spectacle.

? *In which year was the Blue Bell largely built?*

GPS WAYPOINTS

✎	SJ 523 454	**C**	SJ 530 458
A	SJ 524 441	**D**	SJ 526 462
B	SJ 534 451		

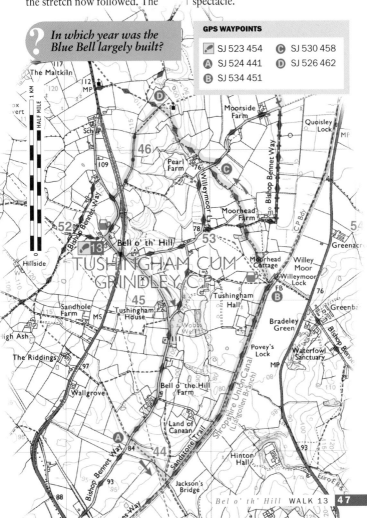

Remain with the towpath past Povey's Lock. The canal runs slightly above the level of Willey Moor. This area, still only partially drained and cultivated, is a remnant of post Ice Age England, thick boulder-clay dotted with low hummocks left as the last ice sheet retreated 15,000 years ago.

B Willeymoor Lock and adjacent tavern are the next target. Immediately before the pub a fingerpost points the way left, down a few steps and beside the beer garden to a kissing-gate. You're on the Sandstone Trail here, so follow the appropriate waymark arrow half-right to a stile above the thatched cottage. Further waymarked stiles beside the driveway take you to the farm road to Moorhead Farm. Go straight across, faithfully following the well-waymarked Sandstone Trail to a minor road.

C Turn right to find a Sandstone Trail fingerpost on the left for Bickleywood and Larkton Hill. Head towards the half-timbered cottage at Pearl Farm, stiles taking you to the right of it. Stay just right of the sunken field road behind the cottage, rising to a stile to the right of trees. Beyond, on a hilltop capped by cedars, is the little old

Old **St Chad's** is remote from any roads, yet still serves as the community's graveyard. A rush-bearing service each summer and occasional services are all that disturb this tiny brick-built church, built in 1689 on an older site. Adjoining it is the hearse-house, still containing the old horse-drawn hearse.

church of St Chad. To reach it, continue up the hillside to a fingerpost beside the graveyard wall.

D Put your back to the churchyard gate and walk ahead up the field to the gates at the top-left corner. Join the lane here and follow it to the main road. Carefully cross into the hedged track and turn left at the end to return to the pub. ●

Old St Chad's Church

Roman Bridge and the Goyt Valley

14

START Ridge Quarry Viewpoint, Marple Ridge

DISTANCE 4½ miles (7.2km)

TIME 2½–3 hours

PARKING Free, 200 yards north of The Romper Inn, Ridge Road, Marple/Strines

ROUTE FEATURES Easy walking on canal towpath, rough lanes and byroads; suitable for dogs

This is an undulating walk down into the Goyt Valley and across a sublime bridge over the river, before picking up old packhorse routes and farm lanes. Reaching a ridge-side track, the route then traverses the fringes of upland pastures to reach the sublime old hamlet of Brook Bottom. Woodland paths and a short taster of canal towpath return you to base and a handy pub.

Turn left from the car park entrance and walk to the first sharp bend. Your way is left here; the building on the right is The Romper Inn. Walk down Hollinwood Lane to reach a bridge over the canal. Cross the bridge and take the steps immediately on the right, rejoining the lane lower down to then continue onto the main road.

A Cross straight over and along the rough lane through Barlow Wood. Bisect the cottages along the narrow path and trace this through to the graceful 'Roman Bridge' spanning the River Goyt. It's given this name due to the style of construction rather than any Latin connection; it probably originated as a packhorse bridge.

Walk beyond it to the rough lane and turn left, remaining with this past the old tollhouse and beneath the high railway viaduct. The old weir here diverted water through to a long-vanished mill complex at Roman Lakes.

PUBLIC TRANSPORT Strines station, on the route, is on the Manchester Piccadilly to Chinley & Sheffield line

REFRESHMENTS Pubs on route and at end; shop in Strines

PUBLIC TOILETS None

ORDNANCE SURVEY MAPS Explorer OL1 (The Peak District, Dark Peak Area)

Remain on the rough road to reach a junction about 200 yds past the lake. Here **B** turn right, almost immediately reaching Bottoms Hall. The rough lane splits here; take the right-hand fork, signed for Cobden Edge on a cast-iron footpath plaque. The old cattle-sheds fall away to the right and this former packhorse route gains height through fine bluebell woods. These soon peel away on the left, revealing Mellor Ridge and its isolated church.

As this rough lane becomes surfaced, keep ahead and follow it up through the golf course. At the top, beside a golf-club car park on your right, turn right along the rougher lane and follow this along the upper edge of the golf course. Rough gorsey pastures stretch away left; to the right are superb views across the Manchester Basin to the Lancashire Moors and Cheshire Plain. Stay on this lane past The Banks Farm.

C Beyond Lily Bank Farm and fold, the lane narrows to a fenced path. Keep left at the isolated cottage to reach the secluded settlement of Brook Bottom, an old weavers' and farming hamlet with a welcoming pub. Just past The Fox Inn take the track on the right, waymarked as the Goyt Way.

This well-used bridlepath winds through woods high above the brook, eventually passing beneath a railway at Strines Station and, later, across the River Goyt to reach a main road (shop to the right here). Go straight across and up the rough lane, passing by cottages to reach a high aqueduct.

Looking towards Whaley Moor from point **C**

D Take the path on the right immediately before this, rising to the Peak Forest Canal towpath. Turn right and walk to the lift-bridge. Cross this and trace the track beyond, to and past a cottage

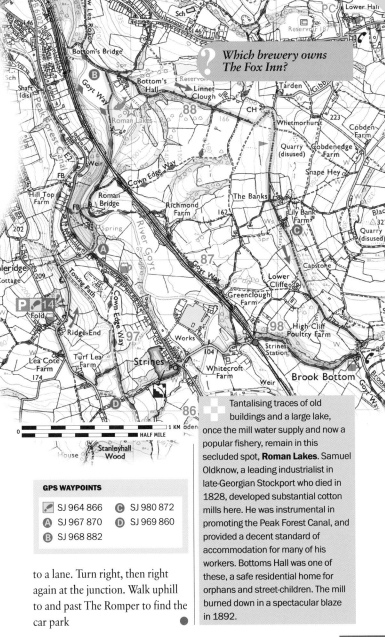

Which brewery owns The Fox Inn?

to a lane. Turn right, then right again at the junction. Walk uphill to and past The Romper to find the car park

Tantalising traces of old buildings and a large lake, once the mill water supply and now a popular fishery, remain in this secluded spot, **Roman Lakes**. Samuel Oldknow, a leading industrialist in late-Georgian Stockport who died in 1828, developed substantial cotton mills here. He was instrumental in promoting the Peak Forest Canal, and provided a decent standard of accommodation for many of his workers. Bottoms Hall was one of these, a safe residential home for orphans and street-children. The mill burned down in a spectacular blaze in 1892.

15 *Kerridge Ridge and the Dean Valley*

START Middlewood Way Car Park, Bollington
DISTANCE 4½ miles (7.2km)
TIME 2½–3 hours
PARKING Free car park off Adlington Road
ROUTE FEATURES Village lanes, field paths and byroads; c. 14 stiles; dogs on leads in fields; one short, steep climb

Starting in the former mill village of Bollington, a short, steep climb gains Kerridge Ridge and follows the Gritstone Trail along this spectacular edge of the Peak District. Falling to Rainow, an old packhorse trail is joined, a wildflower-rich passage along the tranquil valley of the River Dean.

Turn right from the car park entrance and then left into the park. Remain on the right-hand fringe as the tarred path fails; at the far end turn right along the driveway to the main road. Pass beneath the impressive aqueduct, then fork right along Water Street. At the end, turn right to walk uphill to the Red Lion pub. Turn left and cross over.

Ⓐ At the end of the terrace take the waymarked narrow path to the right (not Cow Lane), joining a flagged fieldside path to steps and a kissing-gate. Go ahead-left a few paces to use a handgate; from here turn right up the steep path. Beyond a further kissing-gate go straight over the farm lane, up the steps and onward to the monument.

This strange structure is White Nancy. It was built to commemorate the Battle of Waterloo and is a landmark from miles around. Walk away from this, passing through two kissing gates to pick up the ridge-top Gritstone Trail along Kerridge Ridge for ½ mile.

PUBLIC TRANSPORT Buses to Bollington from Macclesfield and Stockport
REFRESHMENTS Pubs and shops in Bollington and along route
PUBLIC TOILETS At start
ORDNANCE SURVEY MAPS Explorer 268 (Wilmslow, Macclesfield & Congleton)

Countless quarries have bitten into **Kerridge Ridge**; some of these still operate on a small scale after years of dereliction. The sandstone (gritstone is a variety of sandstone) is highly valued for its durability; Coventry Cathedral is paved with it. Small coal mines also littered the steep slopes, once served by tramroads taking these minerals to the Macclesfield Canal, far down to your right.

Much of the length of the Gritstone Trail can be seen; the mast on Sutton Common, The Cloud above Congleton and distant Mow Cop. To your left the rising heights of the Peak District; to your right the Cheshire Plain and, beyond, the mountains of North Wales.

B At the adjoining stile and handgate in a dip, cross through and then bear left, staying on the Gritstone Trail and leaving the ridge top. This green path slopes

> ### What is the logo of the Gritstone Trail?

half-right down to a stile, beyond which take the steeper, left-hand path to a gate-side handgate in the bottom corner. Follow the path; shortly use the handgate up right and trace this woodland path to join an old walled track. Walk down this past the scant remains of Cow Lane Mill then rise up to the main road in Rainow. The Rising

White Nancy

Sun Inn is 150 yds to the right; your way is left.

C Follow the road through the village and 150 yds past the churchyard gates on your right, cross over, fork left (Chapel lane) and keep immediately ahead along Stocks Lane. Walk past the old stocks and pass behind the Robin Hood pub, remaining on this quiet lane to a grassy triangular junction. Rainow once had half-a-dozen cotton mills; the embankment to your right is all that remains of one, Lowerhouse Mill.

Go left at the junction along the bridleway known as Oakenbank Lane. This old packhorse trail winds between secluded meadows above the River Dean, with the imposing Kerridge Ridge to your left. In season, you'll pass great tresses of honeysuckle, banks of foxgloves and rafts of harebells.

D On reaching a curved, walled field-gate entrance on your left take this and go ahead to the trees. Use the handgate (left) and remain on this path (Gritstone Trail again) through several handgates to a lane. Turn left, then first right towards North End Farm. Keep right at the junction. Fork half right off the cattle-grid, aiming downfield for the nearest mill chimney to find a handgate into Cow Lane. Keep ahead to the Red Lion and retrace the initial outward stretch back to the car park.

The east Cheshire Hills from Kerridge Hill

GPS WAYPOINTS

✏ SJ 931 780	Ⓒ SJ 947 757
Ⓐ SJ 936 775	Ⓓ SJ 948 772
Ⓑ SJ 941 762	

16 Church Lawton

START Church Lawton, All Saints Church	

START Church Lawton, All Saints Church

DISTANCE 4¾ miles (7.6km)

TIME 2½ hours

PARKING On the cul-de-sac near the church (signed from the A50)

ROUTE FEATURES Woodland and field paths, towpath; three busy main road crossings; c. 12 stiles; suitable for dogs

Starting in a woodland nature reserve surrounding an old hall, this walk links two of Cheshire's canals, en-route passing through tranquil countryside and offering distant views to Mow Cop and the Gritstone Edge. There are hints, too, of Cheshire's salt heritage and superb wildflowers in spring and summer.

Facing the lychgate, take the waymarked path beside the sheds, right. This soon becomes a wide, gravelled track curving gradually right. Off to the right is Lawton Hall. This vast Georgian pile was latterly a school before becoming derelict. It is now being rebuilt as apartments.

Bear sharp-left with the gravelled path into the woodland nature reserve. As this curves to the lakeshore, keep ahead along the path across the dam. At the dam end take the wider path, slightly left. Huge oak, beech and chestnut line the route; go straight over the farm track and continue to the end of the woods. Go ahead into the cul-de-sac, turn right then keep left to the main road.

🅐 Carefully cross this busy A34 and turn left. In 100 yds go right along Moss Lane; within 30 yds take the low stile on the right, dropping to the towpath. Turn left alongside the Macclesfield Canal. It was completed in 1831 to link the Manchester area more directly with the Midlands. Cotton was a major commodity carried; coal, stone and silk also helped keep the waterway very profitable well into the railway age.

PUBLIC TRANSPORT Buses to Rode Heath from Hanley, Crewe and Alsager

REFRESHMENTS Pub and shop at Rode Heath

PUBLIC TOILETS None

ORDNANCE SURVEY MAPS Explorer 268 (Wilmslow, Macclesfield & Congleton)

The tranquil Macclesfield Canal

Stay with the towpath until you reach a low swing bridge (No. 90) opposite picturesque cottages. Look to the right here, where the folly castle on Mow Cop dominates the horizon. This was built in 1750 for the wealthy Wilbraham family. It straddles the Cheshire/Staffordshire border, and marks the southern end of Cheshire's adventurous Gritstone Trail.

Leave the towpath along the footpath just beyond the cottages. At the lane turn left, then right along Margery Avenue. Where this bends sharp left, take the enclosed path on the right, winding through to a road junction. Take care crossing straight over the two roads here and go along the narrow lane called Claphatches.

B Remain with this until it becomes a grassy path immediately past a cottage. Cross the footbridge and rise gently with this path, ignoring the stile on the right. At the lane cross straight over into Lunts Moss lane, tracing this past cottages and Lunts Moss Farmhouse. About 250 yds past this take the stile on the right into a woodland path. Farther stiles take this path alongside the bluebell woods.

Towpaths are excellent linear nature reserves. Apart from waterside plants, the hedgerows are ablaze with wildflowers in summer. Along this stretch you'll see, among others, campion, foxgloves, ragged robin, woundwort, vetch, cranesbill, comfrey, oxeye daisies and dog roses. Look out, too, for **water voles** – 'Ratty' from *The Wind in the Willows*.

C In a small dip the path forks; here go right into the woods via a stile and sleeper bridge. Beyond the woods follow the direction shown by the waymark on the stile, over a line of four waymarked stiles to reach a lane. Turn right to the main road. Take the second turn left (*cross carefully*), signposted for Sandbach and walk the pavement to the Broughton Arms. Turn left through the car park, cross the bridge and join the Trent and Mersey Canal towpath, water on your left.

Canal milestone

D This is Rode Heath Rise. The tranquil meadows and woods to your right were once a thriving salt works. Brine was pumped to the surface then evaporated and processed before being exported on canal barges to feed Cheshire's chemical industry. Remain on the towpath for $1\frac{1}{2}$ miles to a point 150 yds beyond Lock 47, the top of the Lawton Flight. Take the stile on the left to return to the church. ●

What is a folly?

Macclesfield Canal at Kent Green

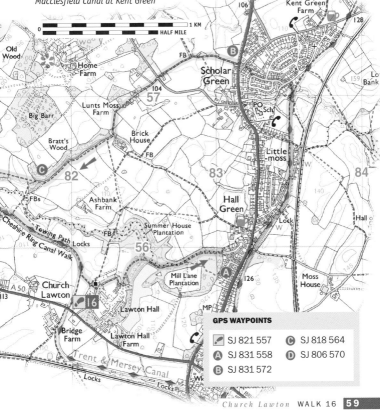

GPS WAYPOINTS

- 🔖 SJ 821 557
- Ⓐ SJ 831 558
- Ⓑ SJ 831 572
- Ⓒ SJ 818 564
- Ⓓ SJ 806 570

17 *Lower Peover*

START Lower Peover Church

DISTANCE 5 miles (8km)

TIME 2½–3 hours

PARKING With consideration, near the church or school on 'The Cobbles' cul-de-sac off the B5081. Or (with permission only) at the adjacent Bells o' Peover pub

ROUTE FEATURES Mostly field paths and back lanes; two busy main road crossings; dogs on leads in pastureland; c. 13 stiles and gates

This walk offers a glimpse of classic Cheshire. From a sublime hamlet with medieval church and ancient inn, the route meanders through wildflower meadows and along peaceful country lanes to Peover Hall, an archetypical Elizabethan country mansion in superb grounds. The return is through rich pasture lands spangled with dewponds and marl-pits and past an old watermill.

Find the kissing-gate at the south-east corner of the churchyard and take the path through the river meadows. Ignore the footbridge and stay on the fieldside path over stiles to gain a lane **A**. Turn left along this. Fork right along Mill Lane; in summer the banks are a mass of fragrant meadowsweet.

Turn right at the T-junction, following Free Green Lane past nurseries to reach a house called Willow Way. Take the stile on the left here and cross the buttercup

Lower Peover church was founded in 1269. The wooden framework and pews within are particularly striking, as is the pleasing mix of sandstone tower and half-timbered body. The church chest came from Norton Priory and is carved from a single piece of 'bog oak', partly fossilised wood recovered from a peat bog 800 years ago. In past times it was a local custom that, in order to prove their strength, girls wishing to marry a local farmer should lift the lid with one hand.

meadow to another stile in line with the greenhouses. Pass behind

PUBLIC TRANSPORT Infrequent buses from Warrington to Lower Peover

REFRESHMENTS Pubs at start and along the route

PUBLIC TOILETS None

ORDNANCE SURVEY MAPS Explorer 268 (Wilmslow, Macclesfield & Congleton)

the tennis court to another stile (the right, waymarked one) and watch your footing here. A path winds along a strip of high grasses and shrubs, past a waymarked post and through to a stile into a road. Carefully cross straight over into Long Lane.

B Simply remain on this quiet byway. After passing a mass of glasshouses the lane gives way to an old cobbled track through fine woods, part of the estate surrounding Peover Hall. Stay on the track to pass a cottage on your left. Upon reaching the three-way fingerpost at the driveway to Peover Hall, take the signed footpath along the 'Private' driveway.

At the ornate gates, go through the left-hand one and along the mossy drive (fingerpost here) opposite and above the impressive stables. As this curves right into the manicured gardens at Peover Hall, your way is left, past the mounting block and through the wrought iron gate, then right to reach a sundial near the gates to St Lawrence's Church.

> **?** *The flags of which two countries are flown from the Bells o' Peover – and what are their names?*

Peover Hall

C Follow the wide path away from the sundial and past the walled garden (on your left) to a kissing-gate at the woodland edge. Go through this and turn left to a stile. Climb this and turn right along the field edge path, soon passing through an area of immature woodland to reach another stile. Take this and turn left along the abandoned driveway through the landscaped parkland. Cross the waist of the lily pond on the gated causeway and trace the tree-lined track to the lodge-house next to the Whipping Stocks Inn.

D *Take extreme care here whilst crossing the A50 road from a point at the telephone box.* Turn right along the verge and then go left along Sandy Lane, signed for Redbrook Farm. Bend right with it and then keep left along the rougher road at the fork, soon passing beside Sandylane Farm. From the roughening lane here are occasional views, on clear days, to the sandstone ridge and, beyond, the mountains of Flintshire, 40 miles away.

GPS WAYPOINTS

✏ SJ 743 741	**C** SJ 772 735
A SJ 746 736	**D** SJ 767 747
B SJ 759 731	**E** SJ 747 743

Keep ahead at the fork, pass through a gate and continue along to and through the old farmyard below Freegreen Farm. Pass straight in front of the imposing farmhouse and along the green path to reach a lane, along which turn right.

E At the next junction turn left along Foxcovert Lane; then in

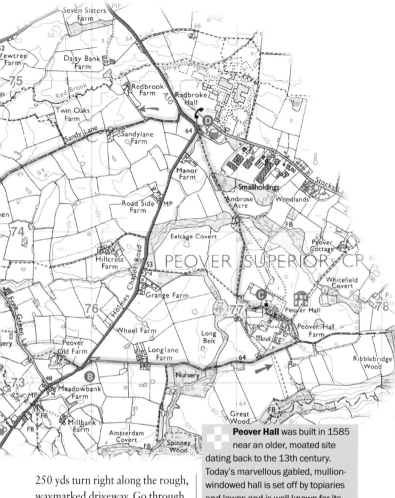

250 yds turn right along the rough, waymarked driveway. Go through the open gateway and down the cobbled lane between houses, then head across the grass entry to a waymarked gateway just past the old Peover Mill. Curve left with the grassy pond-side path to cross a footbridge over the Peover Eye. Turn right to return to the church. ●

Peover Hall was built in 1585 near an older, moated site dating back to the 13th century. Today's marvellous gabled, mullion-windowed hall is set off by topiaries and lawns and is well known for its themed gardens. It's the ancestral home of the Mainwaring family, many of whom are buried in the adjacent church. General Patton lived here for a period during the Second World War. The Hall, stables and gardens are open to the public on Mondays and Thursdays (not Hall) between April and October.

18 *Ogden Clough and Swineshaw*

START Landslow Green, above Stalybridge

DISTANCE 5½ miles (8.8km)

TIME 3 hours

PARKING Hobson Moor Road, Landslow Green. Roadside pull-ins on a no through road

ROUTE FEATURES Field and woodland paths and moorland roads; c. 20 stiles and gates; dogs on leads in sheep country

Here's an easy introduction to moorland walking. The route starts from a peaceful lane serving upland farms before threading through the edge of Hollingworth to a nature reserve created around abandoned reservoirs. Moorland tracks and roads then lead to remote reservoirs high in these south Pennine fringes, before returning via old quarry roads offering magnificent views across the Peak District.

Drive along Hobson Moor Road until it narrows downhill. Park at the roadside here and walk ahead, soon bending right to find Landslow Green Farm on your right. Immediately past this take the gated lane, right, to reach footpath fingerposts. Turn left, cross a stile and walk along the enclosed track. Another stile leads into pasture; keep the wall on your right but dog-leg around the offset corner to find a kissing-gate beyond the stand of trees. Take this gate, then a stile lower down and continue into the farmyard at Thorncliffe Farm.

Swineshaw and Hollingworthall Moor

PUBLIC TRANSPORT None

REFRESHMENTS None on route; pubs and shops in Roe Cross and Mottram

PUBLIC TOILETS none

ORDNANCE SURVEY MAPS Explorer OL1 (The Peak District – Dark Peak)

A Take the farm lane away from the farm, keeping above Thorncliffe Hall (left). Turn left down the rough lane beyond to reach a kissing-gate at the end of the wall on your left. Take this and cross the pasture slightly right to another gate near cottages. Follow the lane to an estate road and turn left.

Stay on this for 250 yds to Cow Lane, left. Ignore this, but take the gap stile on the left immediately beyond the wrought iron gates. At the end of this fenced path turn right above the barns. Swing right beyond these to a fingerpost and a gateway. Take the stile here and join a field-edge path. After the next stile pick up a path beneath oaks, continuing along a muddy path through the edge of woods.

B Climb the ladder stile beyond the brook and head half-left to find a path beneath a vast, low-spreading beech tree. Take the gap beyond (not the Nature Reserve gate) and walk on to a kissing-gate into woods. Cross the brook and, soon afterwards, turn right

What were the reservoirs called and when were they closed?

through the disused gateway to reach a Nature Reserve board.

Just past the board, cross the brook and take the stile beside the field gate. Walk ahead into the grassland for 50 yds and then bear half-right to a kissing-gate in the far corner, re-entering the Nature Reserve. Trace the path through immature woodland, reaching retaining steps just past another Reserve board. Descend these to a spot just above Devil's Bridge across the turbulent brook.

C Do not cross the bridge but, rather, look for the low waymarked post off to the left about 30 yds above the bridge. This narrow path winds up above a side-stream, occasional posts confirming your way. Climb a stile beyond trees into a narrow, steep pasture. Gradually drift to the right of this, curving right with the wall into a walled track. At the end, turn left at the fingerpost, a boggy track bringing you up to an old byre and spring.

D Turn right along the rough road, go through the gate and follow this out into moorland pastures, fine views unfolding to the south-east. Go through the next gate and along the walled track, past ruined buildings to a walker's gate. Walk ahead 50 yds to the low waymarked post and turn left up the moorland road. Stay on this, past another gate to a junction of tracks. Here, remain on your side of the wall and turn right, following the moorland road beneath the line of power cables. Pass a gate eventually to reach a stile/gate into another rough lane. The way is left, but the nearby reservoirs at Swineshaw are a welcome break and often home to wildfowl.

E Pick up the rough track through a very tight kissing-gate, rising to a fingerpost beneath trees. Turn right, pass through the ruins and fork left alongside the wall. This becomes a walled track, with fine views to the right across Manchester. Simply keep the wall close to your left, rising gradually to a gap in a cross-wall. Soon, distant views unfold across the Peak District; the distinctive peaks on the horizon are Mam Tor and Back Tor.

Stick with the wall to find a stile and, just beyond, a sandy quarry road. Bear right along this **F**, remaining on it through a gate to a junction. Keep left here to pass through the complex at Hollingworth Hall. Stay on the main track to reach a tarred lane beyond a Field Centre. Turn right, and at the junction keep ahead along the rougher lane ('Private Road') to return to Hobson Moor Road.

●

Lower Swineshaw Reservoir

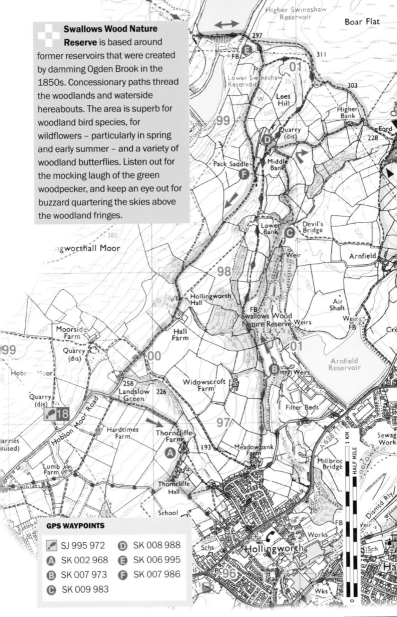

Swallows Wood Nature Reserve is based around former reservoirs that were created by damming Ogden Brook in the 1850s. Concessionary paths thread the woodlands and waterside hereabouts. The area is superb for woodland bird species, for wildflowers – particularly in spring and early summer – and a variety of woodland butterflies. Listen out for the mocking laugh of the green woodpecker, and keep an eye out for buzzard quartering the skies above the woodland fringes.

GPS WAYPOINTS

✍	SJ 995 972	Ⓓ	SK 008 988
Ⓐ	SK 002 968	Ⓔ	SK 006 995
Ⓑ	SK 007 973	Ⓕ	SK 007 986
Ⓒ	SK 009 983		

19 Danebridge and Wincle Minn

START Wincle

DISTANCE 5½ miles (8.8km)

TIME 3½ hours

PARKING Roadside at Danebridge (downhill from The Ship Inn)

ROUTE FEATURES Several sharp climbs, otherwise moderate walking on rough lanes, byroads and paths; muddy in places after rain. c. 20 stiles. Dogs strictly on leads in sheep country

The River Dane and its tributary, Shell Brook, cut deep into the gritstone edge of the Peak District, creating a series of secluded, wooded valleys. This walk explores these, en-route passing hints of former industries and climbing via medieval roadways to the very edge of the National Park, unveiling superb views in all directions from the Gritstone Trail.

 Walk down the drive to the Fishery. Beyond the ponds take the narrow path to the left of the car park entrance at Pingle Cottage. This leads into glorious, secluded meadowland enclosed by hanging woods clothing the Dales's winding gorge, presently reaching a footbridge below a weir.

Ⓐ Cross this, Gig Hall Bridge, and turn right for Barleighford Bridge. These weirs mark the site of Whitelee Mill. They also see the start of a canal leat (feeder); this is followed for the next mile. The leat, here often hardly more than a trickle, flows three miles to Rudyard Lake, created in the 1790s as a header supply for the Caldon Canal.

The path becomes a rough access road; follow it past one stone bridge across the leat to a second, at a padlocked gate beneath pines. Fork right down the tarred lane

> **?** *What is the name of the ship on the pub's sign, and what local connection has it got?*

PUBLIC TRANSPORT None

REFRESHMENTS Pub at start (closed Mondays except BH)

PUBLIC TOILETS None

ORDNANCE SURVEY MAPS Explorer 268 (Wilmslow, Macclesfield & Congleton); also on Explorer OL24 (The Peak District – White Peak area)

here and cross Barleighford Bridge, on the Gritstone Trail.

B Walk uphill 100 yds to the bend; here take the waymarked Gritstone Trail at a stile. Frequent posts keep you on track to gain height across steep pastures. Views stretch across the tranquil valley of Shell Brook to Bosley Cloud, high above Congleton.

The path eventually joins the route of a green road, one of many pre-turnpike routes local historians have identified in this area. Pass the remains of Dumkins Farm and alongside the sunken track to a stile. Turn left this side of it and trace the fence down to a waymarked post. Bear right and drop down to a culvert carrying Shell Brook.

C Follow the steep, winding track beyond, climbing consistently to reach a gate-side handgate. Keep to the left of the field to a handgate, then rise a shade right via another such to the distant Hawkslee Farm. Turn right along the lane, winding up onto Wincle Minn ridge and the reward of enormous views all round.

The lane rises through a gateway. About 100 yds past this, look for a distinct old stoney road sharply back-right. **D** Take this and wind

down to reach the ruins of Mareknowles Farm. Immediately on reaching this, look on the left for a waymark disc on a fence post and take the narrow path outside the old farmyard fence. This soon widens to its guise as another pre-turnpike road. Views up the deep, wooded valley of Shell Brook are superb.

The sunken track drops between old hawthorns to a sharp left bend about 250 yds below the farm. Here, a waymarked post shows the way as right beside an old birch

The old weir at Whitelee Mill

GPS WAYPOINTS

SJ 964 652

A SJ 956 642

B SJ 943 637

C SJ 946 649

D SJ 939 658

E SJ 950 654

and along a good path at the edge of the woods. This drifts left and falls easily down through the woods to a long, slightly kinked wooden footbridge, beyond which climb ahead into the field. Turn left up beneath the line of pylons to join a field road heading for Nettlebeds Farm.

E Just 50 yds shy of the farm is a waymarked post. Turn right, cross the gate-side stile and climb another stile on your left in 50 paces. Trace the hedge, left, through a cross-hedge and then angle half-right to another stile. From here, aim for the right-hand side of the distant farm. A stile and gates take you through the farmyard here at medieval Wincle Grange, an offshoot of Combermere Abbey (near Whitchurch), to a lane. Keep ahead over a cattle-grid. Views of Shutlingsloe and The Roaches are idyllic.

Some 50 yds round the bend take the handgate on the right. Head three-quarters left to a stile into beechwoods. At the foot of the woods, take the drop-stile into pasture, tracing the wall, right, to stiles either side of a driveway. One farther stile across the field meets the lane at The Ship Inn. Turn right for Danebridge.

20 *Three Shires Head*

Three counties meet at a remote, memorable old packhorse bridge spanning the River Dane. This is the focus of pack-routes that criss-crossed the Peak District, taking in salt from Cheshire, fetching out cloth, coal and metals from the dales and moors. The walk, through wooded valleys and across bilberry-clad moorland, also passes evocative remains of industries long reclaimed by nature.

START Peak National Park car park at Clough House, Wildboarclough

DISTANCE 5¾ miles (9.2km)

TIME 3–3½ hours

PARKING Free, at start

ROUTE FEATURES One short, sharp climb, otherwise moderate walking on rough lanes, byroads and paths; walk passes through old quarry workings with loose scree; a few boggy stretches, and c. 10 stiles; dogs strictly on leads in sheep country

With the farm on your right, join the lane and bear right towards Wildboarclough. Shutlingsloe, sometimes called 'The Matterhorn of the Peak', is the shapely hill across the valley. The wooded dale of Clough Brook once echoed to the sound of calico printing and dyeing works and carpet mills, known collectively as Crag Mills. They thrived until the 1860s and declined thereafter, eventually being demolished in the 1950s. Remain on the lane to the junction above Crag Hall; here keep left towards Buxton.

The remains at **Reeve Edge** and **Danebower Quarries** look eerily like old slate quarries but they were, in fact, largely quarried to produce roofing tiles, the shale and mudstone being easy to split along bedding planes. The old chimney was a flue for Danebower Colliery, where coal was mined until the 1920s. The underground levels may have been linked to other remote, local, small-scale collieries by tub-boats on sub-terranean canals, similar to those found at Worsley, in Salford.

? *Which three counties meet at the old packhorse bridge?*

PUBLIC TRANSPORT None

REFRESHMENTS None on route; several country pubs within 1¼ miles of start

PUBLIC TOILETS None

ORDNANCE SURVEY MAPS Explorer OL24 (The Peak District, White Peak area)

A In about 250 yds fork left off the tarred lane along a rough track signed for Three Shires Head, shortly crossing a stile. The wall on your left eventually bends away. At this point veer slightly right to pass close to the isolated little barn, then carefully tackle a boggy area to reach the road. Go straight over and along the path for Turn Edge. This sanded path crosses three sections of duck-boarding; after the last keep right at an indistinct fork to climb a waymarked stile through a ruinous wall. Head half-left from here to the distant Cut-thorn Farm.

To the right are sweeping views across the Dane Valley and Black Brook to the distinctive ridge of The Roaches and isolated Hen Cloud, high above Leek in the Staffordshire Moorlands.

B Cross the lane into the gated, rough old track, one of the many former packhorse roads in this lonely area. This drops into the valley of the River Dane to reach the sublime old packhorse bridge above Panniers Pool. This point is known as Three Shires Head, the bridge is well over 300 years old and the focus of four packhorse trails.

C Cross the main bridge and go directly ahead up the track beyond the metal gate (do not cross the smaller bridge). Immediately before the next bridge and gate fork left, keeping the stream on your right. At the junction of tracks **D** near a wall (about 70 yds before a gate) turn sharp-left back on yourself, joining a grassy moorland track. Curve round with this to join a line of wall on your right.

The old Danebower Colliery

As this wall turns away right, keep ahead to reach the gateway in the distant contour-wall. Turn left here and walk through to the old workings at Reeve Edge Quarries. A waymarked, uneven path through these tumbled workings leads down to stepping-stones across the Dane. Carefully cross them and go straight up the bank to a fingerpost just beyond a circular shooting butt. Turn left to pick up an old quarry road, following this past a pond and up to a gateway above an old chimneystack. Go through the gate and immediately right up the steep path to the main road at a barrier.

E Join the gated bridleway opposite, following it out onto windswept grouse-moors at Dane-bower Hollow. In about ½ mile is an isolated cast-iron footpath sign for Cumberland Brook, provided by the redoubtable Peak and Northern Footpaths Society. Straight on from here for another half a mile is England's second-highest pub, The Cat and Fiddle, at 1,690 feet beaten only by the Tan Hill Inn in North Yorkshire – another Cheshire surprise.

Our way, however, is left here; on clear days views extend across Shutlingsloe to the Welsh Mountains, south to the Wrekin in Shropshire and east across the Peak District. The path crosses to the right-hand bank of the infant Cumberland Brook; then crosses this below a small waterfall eventually to reach a rough road and gateway.

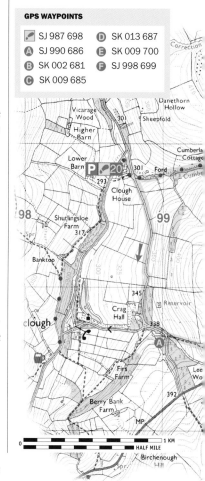

GPS WAYPOINTS

🖊 SJ 987 698   **D** SK 013 687
A SJ 990 686   **E** SK 009 700
B SK 002 681   **F** SJ 998 699
C SK 009 685

F The small Danethorn Colliery once thrived here. Turn downstream, climb the stile and trace this track down below the isolated Cumberland Cottage and over a footbridge to return to the lane above Clough House. ●

The summer months see a wide variety of birds using these moorland pastures as their home. **Skylarks** and **meadow pipits** are the most common, but keep an ear out for the **curlew**, its melancholy call a haunting memory of these uplands. The colourful **wheatear** is a frequent visitor, and look out for **dippers** and **wagtails** along the fast flowing streams. A whirring of wings and distinct 'go-back' call means you'll have all-but trodden on a **red grouse**, masters of camouflage in the thick heather.

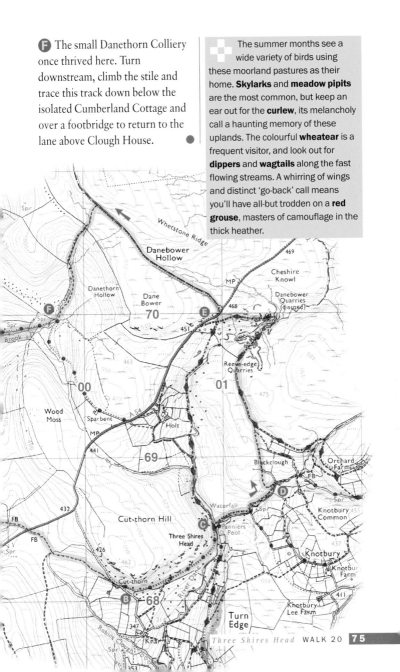

Further Information

Walking Safety

Always take with you both warm and waterproof clothing and sufficient food and drink. Wear suitable footwear, i.e. strong walking boots or shoes that give a good grip over stony ground, on slippery slopes and in muddy conditions. Try to obtain a local weather forecast and bear it in mind before you start. Do not be afraid to abandon your proposed route and return to your starting point in the event of a sudden and unexpected deterioration in the weather.

All the walks described in this book will be safe to do, given due care and respect, even during the winter. Indeed, a crisp, fine winter day often provides perfect walking conditions, with firm ground underfoot and a clarity of light unique to that time of the year. The most difficult hazard likely to be encountered is mud, especially when walking along woodland and field paths, farm tracks and bridleways – the latter in particular can often get churned up by cyclists and horses. In summer, an additional difficulty may be narrow and overgrown paths, particularly along the edges of cultivated fields. Neither should constitute a major problem provided that the appropriate footwear is worn.

Bollington from Kerridge End

The old boathouse at Capesthorne

Follow the Country Code

- Enjoy the countryside and respect its life and work
- Guard against all risk of fire
- Take your litter home
- Fasten all gates
- Help to keep all water clean
- Keep your dogs under control
- Protect wildlife, plants and trees
- Keep to public paths across farmland
- Take special care on country roads
- Leave livestock, crops and machinery alone
- Make no unnecessary noise
- Use gates and stiles to cross fences, hedges and walls

(The Countryside Agency)

The Roman Bridge, Marple

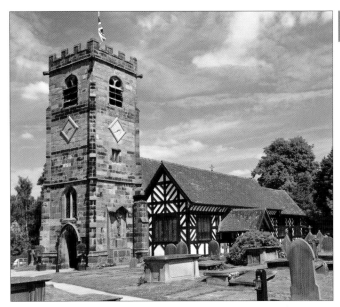

Lower Peover church

Congleton: 01260 271095
Ellesmere Port & Neston:
0151 356 5562
Macclesfield: 01625 504114
Nantwich: 01270 537359
Northwich: 01606 353500
Runcorn: 01928 576776
Warrington: 01925 442180

Public Transport

For all enquiries about local bus
services in Cheshire call
Traveline on
0871 200 2233.
For rail enquiries call:
0845 484950.

Ordnance Survey Maps

Explorer OL1 (The Peak District –
Dark Peak area), Explorer OL24
(The Peak District – White Peak
area), Explorer 257 (Crewe
&Nantwich), Explorer 266 (Wirral
& Chester), Explorer 267
(Northwich & Delamere Forest),
Explorer 268 (Wilmslow,
Macclesfield & Congleton),
Explorer 276 (Bolton, Wigan &
Warrington)

Answers to questions

Walk 1: 12.
Walk 2: A form of public

punishment used until Victorian times. Minor criminals and nuisance-makers would have their feet securely locked into this frame, allowing villagers to ridicule them and even throw rotten vegetables, and other things, at the offender.

Walk 3: 74 pits.

Walk 4: A friend of Alderley Edge now living in California, 1961.

Walk 5: 1784. The date is to be seen above a doorway near to the foot of the mill chimney.

Walk 6: The Peak District National Park.

Walk 7: Christmas Day, 1972.

Walk 8: English Heritage.

Walk 9: The River Weaver Navigation.

Walk 10: 2008.

Walk 11: Before steam engines and diesel motors took over, canal boats were towed along by sturdy boat horses, attached to the bow (front) of the boat by a long rope and harness. The wide path found alongside canals is thus known as the towpath.

Walk 12: 82 years (completed in 1359).

Walk 13: 1667; the date is above the porch doorway.

Walk 14: Robinson's Brewery.

Walk15: A black boot with a yellow G within it, all on a yellow waymark arrow or disc.

Walk 16: It is a building with no particular purpose other than to appeal to the whim of the person paying for its construction. They are often in the form of castle ruins or towers; most date from the 18th and 19th centuries.

Walk 17: The UK and the USA; known as The Union Jack and The Stars and Stripes.

Walk 18: Wastelodge and Hollingworth Reservoirs were closed in 1987.

Walk 19: The ship is the *Nimrod*. It was a ship used on one of Sir Ernest Shackleton's polar voyages in the early 1900s and was captained by Sir Philip Brocklehurst, who lived in nearby Swythamley Hall.

Walk 20: Cheshire, Staffordshire and Derbyshire

Lymm village